TEXTILES AND TOIL

Hadden's Mill (1798–1901) in the Green at foot of Windmill Brae. Site now occupied by Littlewoods Stores.

TEXTILES AND TOIL

The Factory System and the Industrial Working Class in Early 19th Century Aberdeen

by

ROBERT DUNCAN

ABERDEEN CITY LIBRARIES

© Aberdeen City Libraries
1984
ISBN 0 946920 02 8

PRINTED **AUP** ABERDEEN

CONTENTS

INTRODUCTION

NOTE ON SOURCES

In the interests of readability, scholarly apparatus, foot-notes and references have deliberately been kept down to a minimum. For the further information of those readers who may wish to consult the parliamentary papers used in this study, Aberdeen University Library has a full set of copies. These are conveniently available in the facsimile edition reprinted by Irish University Press and appear under the heading 'Industrial Revolution'. Other and secondary sources dealing with the locality may be consulted in the Local Collections at Aberdeen University Library and the City Public Library. I am indebted to the librarians at both centres for their help and co-operation.

INTRODUCTION

It is a duty, do it who may—and it shall be done—to expose the factory system of that day, as it stood in our 'moral north'. Fairly to put the knife into the dead monster, lay bare its dark core, dissect it in broad day, that the world may see who had the fat and who the famine portion of that heartless trading.

> William Thom, *Rhymes and
> Recollections of a Hand Loom Weaver,*
> ed. W. Skinner (1880), p. 2.

The Aberdeen weaver poet was only one voice among many from different walks of life who passionately condemned the factory system. Throughout the country, various indictments of the factory system appeared in a welter of journalism, pamphlets, books, and official parliamentary enquiries. In Aberdeen and elsewhere, clergymen and Tory humanitarians were outraged by the inhumane aspects of the system, the exploitation and degradation of young workers. In a startling metaphor which was also used later by Karl Marx in his classic critique of industrial capitalism (*Das Kapital*, Everyman edition (1930), pp. 713-14), the Tory *Aberdeen Journal* issued this editorial statement on 23 January 1833, after reading the report of the Select Committee on the Factories Bill:

> It was with horror and loathing that we perused the evidence. Commerce seems like the Car of Juggernaut, rolling onwards, in triumph and in pride, over the mangled limbs and mutilated bodies of its victims.

However, despite such damning indictments, modern historians are divided in their evaluation of the reliability of the evidence, particularly the evidence submitted to parliamentary enquiries of the time. Some historians maintain that much of the evidence against the factory system is distorted and exaggerated, painting a universally black picture. Others take a different view, allowing for the existence of favourable exceptions to the rule, but otherwise claiming that the regime created by industrial capitalism undeniably committed new levels of wholesale violence against more than one generation of working people. This short study of the factory system in Aberdeen supports the second viewpoint and is based upon the weight of available evidence. In addition, the approach is unashamedly influenced by the work and methods of Frederick Engels' *The Condition of the Working Class in England* (1844, and reprinted in modern editions) and of Edward Thompson's *Making of the English Working Class* (1963). It is left to the reader to consult these texts, to participate in the continuing controversy, and to make up his or her mind on this crucial historical issue.

One of the purposes of writing this essay was to close a yawning gap in local history. For all the books and articles produced in recent years by widely-read and popular local historians and writers such as Fenton Wyness, Cuthbert Graham, G M Fraser and Alexander Keith, none of these gentlemen appear to have considered it a worthwhile project to examine the life and labour of the Aberdeen working class, its experiences and struggles. This short study of the factory system may help to redress the neglect and hopefully may appeal to the interested public, not least to the many teachers and pupils in secondary schools in Aberdeen and the North East.

by Robert Duncan

1

SOCIAL CHANGE AND THE CREATION OF A WORKING CLASS

It will be seen that next to the families of persons actually working in the factories, the most unhealthy are those of weavers and labourers. I believe it will be found to be the case that nearly all the wives of weavers, and many of those of labourers, formerly worked in factories; and even giving the circumstances of low wages and consequent domestic privations their due weight, I think we have reason to fear that the descendants of those persons are physically deteriorating.

> remarks of A C Kilgour, doctor of medicine in Aberdeen, contained in *Factories Enquiry Commission. Second Report*, Parliamentary Papers 1833

I have observed in the course of my practice many families employed at factories fed on a few very indifferent potatoes with a little salt (for dinner), and then hurried off to work. The effects of such diet were a large number of cases of stomach complaints, scrofula etc. The evil effects do not stop here: the husband drinks the worst of spirits on the way to his work; his wife gets notice of this circumstance, and she retaliates upon her husband with similar conduct, while the effects of this united debauching is, that no food is able to be provided for days; the younger branches of the family are now obliged to go to the street to steal or to prostitute themselves, and the result often is, that their lives are either sacrificed to disease or to the laws of their country.

I may here mention, that too little attention is given to the miserable state of their apparel and bed-clothes in the winter season, which is attended with baneful consequences to their existence, considering the heated state of the rooms in which they work through the day.

> Alexander Fraser, surgeon to the Aberdeen General Dispensary, submitting opinion to *Factories Enquiry Commission. First Report*, Parliamentary Papers 1833

Aberdeen in the late eighteenth century was still small and compact, but already its areas of settlement and population were growing steadily. Most of its people lived within the central parish of St Nicholas, in St Clements parish down to the tiny fishing community of Footdee, and behind the Castlehill to the east and north. By the turn of the century, the urban area was extending to the north and west, within the large straggling parish of Old Machar. This comprised the Gilcomston district and Denburn, quite near the centre of the city, and was inhabited for the most part by colonies of artisan weavers and shoemakers who had chosen to settle there ostensibly because house rents were lower than in St Nicholas. The communities of hand-loom weavers lived in Jack's Brae, Shortloanings, Leadside, and along the lower Denburn, all within the Rosemount area. Further out, at Woodside and Cotton, growing settlements housed a distinctly separate community of working-class incomers who were engaged at the Donside textile mills.

As large-scale textile industry developed at Donside and in the city by the first decades of the nineteenth century, Aberdeen grew at an unprecedented rate.[1] Census figures (to the nearest thousand) indicate a remarkable increase of population:

Year					
1801	1811	1821	1831	1841	1851
Population					
27,000	35,000	44,000	57,000	63,000	72,000

By 1821, Aberdeen was thirteenth-largest town in Britain in terms of population, and fourth in Scotland. And although Dundee had surpassed it by the 1840s, Aberdeen was until that time the major industrial centre for textile production north of Lanarkshire.

Textiles dominated the Aberdeen economy in the early nineteenth century. At the highest point of production in the mid-1830s the combined textile industries provided employment for approximately 13,000 men, women, and children—or almost a quarter of the population.

Even though this statistic is an impressive one, it would nevertheless be wrong to characterise Aberdeen as a mill town, densely packed with factories and showing a skyline of chimney stacks. Indeed, Aberdeen was far from being a single occupation town, its expanding economy and social structure containing considerable diversity. A breakdown of employment in the branches of textiles reveals an obvious picture by the 1840s. Linen alone engaged 7000 workers, cotton over 4000, and between 2500 and 3000 workers in the woollen and carpet-making industries. Thus the mill worker was the most conspicuous figure in the employment landscape; but alongside thousands of workers involved in the other sectors of growth in the local economy, particularly in the various construction industries. Extensive programmes of civic improvement launched by 'city fathers' like the Haddens and their successors created a building boom and work for a host of stone quarrymen, paviours, cutters, polishers, masons and general building labourers, all employed in labour-intensive occupations.

Aberdeen was also a major centre of shipbuilding. No fewer than six flourishing shipyards at Footdee employed hundreds of wrights, carpenters and moulders. In connection with shipping, several small firms employed over 200 workers in 1840 in the making of rope, cord and twine. By the same date, the growing machine engineering industry, iron founding and repairing provided work for over 1000 skilled and semi-skilled men. Other new industries started in the eighteenth century were gradually enlarged, notably comb and paper making. Three paper mills, situated outside the city, were still on a small scale, but the comb works employed nearly 400 workers, mostly children and adolescents.

Mention of these new industries and crafts should, however, not obscure the prominent features of the surviving, older economy which also had to expand to cater for the needs of Aberdeen's ever-growing population. For instance, according to the classifications and figures in the 1841 Census return, traditional artisan occupations made up a large section of the labour force. Artisan society was headed by over 4000 hand-loom weavers in the 1800s (but, as we shall see later, a craft in rapid decline and disintegration over the years); followed by 800 boot and shoemakers, over 600 carpenters and joiners, 500 tailors, 500 blacksmiths and around 200 cabinet-makers and upholsterers.

Within these artisan trades, there was a marked contrast in general conditions, wages, hours and social prospects. The likes of shipwrights, mechanics, engineers and masons were, on the whole better off than the struggling hand craft shoemakers, tailors and handloom weavers who belonged to trades which were under pressure from unscrupulous masters and the whip of competition. Among the lowest paid and most exploited sections of the work force were female domestic servants, regarded as a cut above the mill girl. By 1841, Aberdeen's growing middle class was employing more than 3500 domestic servants as rich and fashionable society moved away from the city centre to new houses in the developing west end beyond Union bridge.

The growth of Aberdeen into the regional capital of the North East, and major commercial, service and industrial centre, attracted and required an incoming working population. The first generations of the new urban working class were recruited mainly from the parishes of Aberdeenshire and also from the adjoining counties. Aberdeen's incomers by 1840 included little more than 1000 Irish and an unknown but small number of people from Highland areas. Thus the population was fairly homogeneous, the 1841 Census report for the city and suburbs revealing that three out of four of the inhabitants had been born within the county as against migrants from more distant areas.

Most of these incomers came from the land, uprooted by the agricultural revolution which transformed farming methods and the old ways of rural life. Improving lairds reorganised their estates and made them into profitable concerns, producing livestock, dairy goods, cereal and root crops for sale in wider markets. There is sufficient evidence from the First and Second Statistical Accounts of the 1790s and 1830s respectively to show that in many country parishes in Aberdeenshire and the North East generally, large numbers of small tenants and cottars were not absorbed by the changes in farming and were surplus to the needs of the landowner. Sooner or later, such tenants were persuaded or forced to leave their holdings and move away to places where they could seek a new life. The poor peasantry were caught out between the revolution in farming on one hand, and by developments in the local textile industry on the other. Unable to draw a sufficient living from the land under the traditional system of farming, they had depended upon additional earnings from knitting stockings, spinning yarn, and hand-loom weaving. However, as the next section explains, these sources of earnings were rapidly being eroded as Aberdeen industrialists no longer found it profitable and convenient to employ the services of large numbers of domestic outworkers. In the circumstances, those dependent rural families had virtually no option but to leave, and many of them may well have been attracted into the Aberdeen area in the expectation of regular work and better living standards.

Few of these incomers could yet begin to comprehend the grim reality that awaited them as new members of the working class in a city and suburbs in the throes of great transformation. Thousands of families were about to encounter another kind of squalor and meagre life in overcrowded, disease-infested tenements and courts, as planned housing provision was non-existent. Housing for the working class in the city was deficient and insanitary. The incoming industrial labour force found rented accommodation where they could, often among the disreputable poor who inhabited the east and the centre, in the mean lanes and wynds of the Vennel, leading from Gallowgate to George Street, in the dens of vice around Peacock's Close, Pensioners' Close and Smith's Court near Castlehill, and in Putachieside—a slum area 'inhabited by a poor and uncomfortable population, with hosts of squalling children', not to be removed until the Market Street developments of the 1840s,[2] The appalling conditions of tenement life were revealed in official investigations, particularly in the sanitary enquiry of 1842. Overcrowding was rife in the centre of the city, and at the worst, up to eight people lived in one room, 'with every crevice stopped'. Only working-class families with 'young men working as tradesmen were able to afford the rent for sometimes three apartments, each with its one or two beds'. Unscrupulous private landlords had a field day, taking advantage of the great demand for rented housing, and by the 1840s, 'in conseqence of the frequency of arrears, a practice is creeping in of collecting the rents in small sums weekly, and a class of landlords in this way contrive to obtain a much higher rent than their premises are worth'.[3] At Woodside and Grandholm, the housing situation was not so desperate, as paternalistic, factory-owning lairds provided rented accommodation for their incoming workers; but, for the majority of immigrant families coming into the Aberdeen area, there was no prospect of decent housing even if there was plenty of work.

TEXTILES: THE RISE OF INDUSTRIAL CAPITALISM AND THE FACTORY SYSTEM

Unlike central Scotland, Aberdeen and the North East lacked coal and iron deposits and avoided the concentrated development of heavy industry from the end of the eighteenth century. This meant that the area and its population escaped the ravages of coal mining, iron workings and slag heaps. Instead, the principal sector of the industrial revolution in Aberdeen during the early nineteenth century was in the manufacture of a range of textile goods from wool, flax and cotton, giving rise to enormous social and economic changes.

Before the transition to industrial capitalism and large scale production of textiles, Aberdeen and the North East generally already had a long connection with the production of woollen and linen goods.[1] This activity, above all, had laid the economic foundations of Aberdeen as a thriving commercial and shipping centre in the eighteenth century. In Aberdeen, many of its 27,000 people in 1800 were engaged in the preparation, production and export of woollens and linen thread. By far the most important export commodity was stockings, a quality product which had gained Aberdeen an international reputation. These were domestic industries, organised by more than a score of prosperous Aberdeen merchants. The biggest textile entrepreneur in the later eighteenth century was James Hadden whose business in woollens extended far into the rural hinterland of the North East. He used agents to supply thousands of country people with wool, mainly cottar women who prepared the shanks and knitted them up into stockings and mitts. These women were paid on a piece-work basis for each article. The agents collected in the finished products and then took them into Aberdeen for packing and marketing.[2]

This 'putting out' system also operated in the domestic linen industry, where country women spun from flax after the fibre had been prepared by flaxdressers, or hecklers, as they were called. The bulk of this thread was then transported into Aberdeen for export. Most country cottages had a spinning wheel, worked by the women and girls; and many were also fitted up with a hand loom, the weaving usually being done by the man. When they were not making garments for their own families or for sale to local customers, they were employed by the likes of Aberdeen merchants. Such domestic occupations had long been a source of part-time earnings (full-time for some men) in Aberdeen and the households of rural families throughout Aberdeenshire and beyond.

However, although the domestic system in knitted stockings and mitts continued to provide some employment for female labour until well into the nineteenth century—as late as the 1840s the Hadden firm supplied worsted to women in landward parishes such as Echt and Leochel-Cushnie—this pattern of economic activity was falling away and was increasingly being replaced from the turn of the century as the scattered network of extensive, but small-scale domestic production was overtaken in stages by the development of industrial capitalism and intensive large-scale production in and around Aberdeen.[3] This brought the concentration of production into the new framework of the factory as revolutionary power-driven machinery was introduced, firstly in the spinning process by the 1790s and in weaving by the 1820s.

In the Aberdeen area, as elsewhere, the pioneering phases of industrialisation in textiles had their share of growing pains, trial and error, and successful breakthrough. Some leading historians give the 1780s as the decade of 'take-off' into the textile revolution, and this may be accurate for the British experience as a whole; but in the Aberdeen locality, there was no sudden acceleration into sustained industrial growth until the 1820s, when important factory extensions were made and when steam-driven power looms were successfully introduced into weaving.

Prior to the application of steam power for machinery, the early factories depended upon the availability of water power. This helps to explain why the first factories were situated on the banks of the river Don, in rural settings at Woodside and Persley, nearly three miles from the city. Here, the pioneering achievements of the landowners and merchants who became industrialists were as enterprising as any in the kingdom.

One of the earliest, largest, and technologically most advanced cotton mills built in Scotland was the Woodside Works, started in 1779. This was the property of the progressive laird and burgh reformer Patrick Barron who at first enlisted the help of the famous inventor and factory master Richard

Woodside Works. Established, 1779, by Gordon, Barron & Co., closed during the depression of the 1840's. Buildings taken over by Pirie & Sons, papermakers, of Stoneywood Works.

Arkwright. The water frame for spinning cotton calicoes, skilled mechanics and managers were introduced and recruited from Arkwright's mills in Derbyshire. By the 1790s it was a giant undertaking by the standards of the day, containing a six-floor building for water-power spinning and two big weaving sheds fitted up with two hundred looms.[4] The firm of Gordon, Barron and Company was the only cotton manufacturer in the Aberdeen area until the 1800s when wartime demand led to the speculative formation of several small companies. These, however, were short-lived owing to lack of capital resources, technical and managerial shortcomings, and the disastrous effects of Napoleon's Continental System which blockaded the import of British manufactured goods into Europe.

The Woodside Works was the largest factory built at Donside in the eighteenth century and was to remain so until the trade depression of the 1840s put it out of business. Three other textile factories had been built at Donside before 1800. The most significant was the linen-making firm of Leys, Masson and Company situated at Grandholm, and a close neighbour of the Woodside cotton giant on the opposite bank. Started in 1749, it became one of the largest flax spinning mills in Britain. By the 1800s it was a five-storey building containing two hundred and forty spinning frames, and there were also several outbuildings where over 1500 hand-loom weavers worked. Here, as at the Woodside Works, water wheels were used quite early on to drive the carding machines and spinning frames.

Also at Donside, and built before 1800, two flax and worsted spinning mills were situated at Gordon's Mills, with a combined total of about seven hundred workers.

However, in and immediately around the city, industrial capitalism in textiles was not noticeable until about 1800. It was only when steam power was successfully applied to spinning that it was possible to build factories and mills away from riverside areas. Thus, one large woollen factory, and several large linen and cotton factories, all using steam power, became part of the city landscape in the first two decades of the nineteenth century. Hadden's woollen factory at the Green, built up to five storeys in the 1790s, was at that time fitted up with spinning jennies and carding machines supplied by power from steam engines. Two flax spinning mills soon followed. Milne, Cruden and Company were established at Spring Garden, and a small mill built at Broadford, bought over by an English industrialist and Tory M P John Maberley, was first extended in the 1810s for the spinning of yarn and patent thread by steam-power.

Within the structure of industrial capitalism in the Aberdeen locality, the linen industry took pride of place, with cotton not far behind in second place. Apart from the early start made by Gordon, Barron and Co at Woodside, other cotton spinning and weaving firms appeared in Aberdeen from the 1800s. In 1800 at Poynernook, near the harbour, Forbes and Low set up a cotton spinning mill equipped with steam-power. By the 1830s it employed six hundred workers, and was slightly larger than the other newly-built cotton works—the Bannermill—situated on the links from 1826. Meanwhile, Gordon, Barron and Co set up another cotton weaving premises at Belmont Street (where William Thom the celebrated weaver poet worked and suffered for seventeen years) but which collapsed in the depression of 1830. This was a hand-loom weaving premises at Belmont Street, and only a small extension into the city by the enlarged and integrated Woodside Works which by the 1820s was able to handle all the processes in cotton manufacture, from the preparation of the raw material to power-loom weaving and scientific methods of coloured finishing. By then the Woodside Works employed nearly 3000 workers.

The application of steam-power weaving in cotton, at the Woodside Works, and first of all in 1824 at the Broadford linen works, removed the bottle-neck which for over thirty years had separated mechanised spinning and weaving. The development of water power and then of steam power in spinning had resulted in the production of enormous amounts of yarn which had created regular work and prosperity for thousands of hand-loom weavers working in their own homes or in workshops. But the fortunes of the hand-loom weavers were reversed dramatically from the 1820s once the introduction of steam-power looms in the factory destroyed their profession. Thus in linen and cotton, and also in the major woollen firm of the Haddens which by the 1830s was specialising in the making of worsted carpets, the various stages of preparation and production were completed in factories and workshops in and around the city, effectively dealing a death blow to the putting-out and domestic system and ensuring that large-scale, speeded-up production became the norm.

The pioneering industrialists in the Aberdeen area were with one exception, all local men. Much of the capital for industry came from improved landed estate, as in the case of Patrick Barron and Thomas Leys. They formed partnerships with merchants who were already involved in established wool and thread trades. In this way, the Hadden family of textile entrepreneurs, having started from obscurity in mid-eighteenth century Aberdeen, became linked in business with the Leys family who were landed gentry. Inter-marriage secured these links, connecting the Haddens and Leys, while the Bannermans were linked with the Milnes by both business and marriage. These factory masters were prominent within the local ruling elite, although they did not share the same political views. This elite provided the political and public leadership throughout the early nineteenth century. In the era before the passing of the 1832 Reform Act, the Tories were in power, with the Hadden family holding a near monopoly of control in the municipal corporation. James Hadden served four times as provost, and his younger brother three times prior to 1832.

The Haddens and the Leys did most to reshape the centre of Aberdeen, presiding over the levelling of St Katherine's Hill to make way for Union Street in 1800, and for other thoroughfares leading in and out of the city. Thomas Bannerman and his son Alexander championed the Whig-liberal interest in opposition to the Tories, and when Aberdeen was made a constituency in 1832, Alexander Bannerman was elected as its first MP.

Of all the leading textile firms in the community, the Broadford works was an exception in that it was owned and managed by Englishmen. Thomas Maberley was already a factory owner in Edinburgh, Glasgow, and in the Dundee area before he took over Broadford in the 1810s. Maberley never resided in the city, and the driving force in the Broadford flax spinning and weaving firm was his nephew Stephen Pellatt, manager of the firm until his death in 1839. When the Maberley enterprise collapsed in 1830, Richards and Co became the owners, with Pellatt staying on as manager.[5] As will be seen later, Pellatt was to gain a notorious reputation among the workers as a ruthless manager. At Broadford, the work discipline was at its most oppressive, and if one also considers the business and family links which created a solidarity of interests among the other factory masters in the neighbourhood, the workers were indeed justified in contending that they were faced by a 'combination of masters' when struggling to get better wages and conditions in the 1830s and 1840s.

3

DIVISION OF LABOUR: MEN, WOMEN, AND CHILDREN

Textile factory workers in Aberdeen were predominantly young and female, and teenage mill girls were the most conspicuous and numerous body of female workers in and around the city. In common with their counterparts elsewhere, Aberdeen factory masters committed themselves as far as practicably possible to the policy of excluding adult males from the operation of spinning and weaving machines. They reckoned that young female operatives would be cheaper to employ as well as being easier to discipline to regular work. Thus there were few factory jobs for grown men. However, in the early stages of mechanised spinning, considerable muscle-power was needed to work the mules, and male operatives were employed as mule spinners at the Woodside cotton works. As machines were improved and adapted, young females were brought in to replace male spinners. At other factories and mills in the area, it was standard practice from the beginning to employ females as spinners.

Men were employed in several capacities in the linen mills. For instance, skilled flax dressers combed out and prepared the raw material. These hecklers worked in close, dust-filled sheds attached to the mills. Slubbers drew out and twisted the flax prior to spinning and tenters served as machine supervisors and skilled mechanics at all the factories. Many ancillary workers were men, employed as sorters, packers, and carters. Finally the most obvious male preserve was the job of foreman and overseer on the factory floor.

Nevertheless, they were greatly outnumbered by mill girls, and particularly by young spinners. For every spinner, there was at least one piecer to attend the spinning frame. Boy and girl piecers were usually younger than the typical teenage spinner, and they were responsible for spotting and tying broken and loose threads. Piecers also cleaned the machinery, even—as at Gordon's Mills—when it was still in motion. Children were also given the 'easy' jobs of carrying bobbins and filling crates, lifting them from floor to floor.

There is ample evidence to show that children were employed at an early age in Aberdeen textile factories. Until the first effective Factory Act in 1833, there was no law preventing the use of child labour below the age of nine in textile factories. Before this date, it is not possible to ascertain precisely the extent to which the Aberdeen factory masters practised and encouraged the employment of children under this age, although there are several known instances. Evidence given by Aberdeen factory masters before the parliamentary enquiry in 1833 contains some ambiguous statements, but points to the use of child labour. For example, the stated policy at the Poynernook cotton mill had always been to exclude children below the age of ten, but most masters admitted to the practice of taking on younger children. Thomas Bannerman said that nine was the normal minimum age of entry into his factory but did not say whether he resisted the pleas of parents who 'often press for employment to younger ones'.[1] One owner who did admit to this practice was James Kilgour from the Woodside Works: 'At the urgent request of parents or near relatives, younger children have been taken in as an act of charity.' Further, Thomas Leys Hadden from the Grandholm said that 'ten years is the lowest age at which we employ children, but in some few instances they may be under that age'. And while he considered it unnecessary to employ children below the age of twelve, he nevertheless was prepared to do so, allegedly on compassionate grounds, 'chiefly to oblige poor parents who live in the neighbourhood of the works, and who cannot otherwise support them'. Hadden liked to appear as a fatherly figure, and was satisfied that his conscience was clear on this issue.

From Samuel Smiles' biography of Thomas Edward, it is possible to draw a closer picture of child labour at the Grandholm about 1820. Thomas was nine when he went to work there. A youngster could progress through a hierarchy of jobs, earning a little more in wages each time. At first, he was put into the heckling shed as an apprentice flaxdresser, starting at 3s. a week. He was then transferred to the spinning mill to become a case lifter, and soon afterwards graduated to the carding room where he had to attend two carding machines which prepared the yarn for spinning. Finally, by the time he was eleven, he moved up to the roving room alongside the spinners, and was earning 6s. a week.[2]

From Smiles' account, we are told that Thomas and his brother chose to work there as it paid better than other jobs in the city. This explanation may be unreliable in several respects, but at least the likes of Thomas and his brother were not forced into the factory as bound boy apprentices. In other parts of the country, orphan children were often put out to factory work by the poor law authorities and there are many accounts of their ill-treatment. Such pauper apprentices were forced labour in the early years of industrialisation when it was difficult to persuade adults to become factory workers. Apparently, only one Aberdeen textile factory participated in this scheme—at the Woodside cotton works until about 1803. Here, bound boys were apprenticed to calico printing and for a time they lived in a castellated building situated on the south side of the Don, near Persley Bridge. Built by Gordon, Barron and Co in 1797, it was known as 'The Barracks', a nickname which may convey some impression not only of the appearance of the place but of the regime that existed there. By 1803, the building was no longer being used for this purpose; houses were being built for factory workers in the village, and indentured labour was on the way out.

Employers agreed about the advisability and the necessity of engaging young workers: they were cheap labour and could be moulded into disciplined and regular work from an early age. With the exception of some aspects of linen weaving, the machine operative did not need to exercise great physical strength to work a frame or a loom,; attentive eyes, dexterity of hands and fingers, and the mental and physical capacity to persevere for long hours standing over the machine, were the most essential requirements. As Alex Cooper, manager at Grandholm explained in 1833, young girls could be trained up to the art of spinning, preferably from an early age:

> From ten to twelve years is the best time to teach a child to spin, and it takes from three to four years to make a good spinner. It is much more expensive to teach them at a later age, because they take as long to learn, and during all that time require larger wages.[3]

In time, machines were converted and simplified for young females to attend. By the 1820s and 1830s girls and women were operating the spinning mules at all the cotton works. The economic rationale behind this conversion was stated frankly by Kilgour, cotton manufacturer:

Grandholm Works. Built, 1797, on north side of Don by Leys, Masson and Co., owners of Gordon Mills. Passed, 1859, to Crombie family, under whose name it still trades.

Fewer grown up people would be required. Improvements in machinery are made with a view to the greatest possible produce at the lowest rate of wages, and as soon as practicable to supersede manual labour.[4]

If these juvenile spinners and reelers did not leave to get married, and managed somehow to keep clear of severe injury or illness, they could remain in their occupation until late middle age, although such women were always in a minority. Few women could have lasted as long as Betty Robinson, who, aged fifty-three in 1833, had been a reeler in the Poynernook cotton mill for twenty-six years

and has always worked on the same spot. Last year, the floor on which she stood so long was found to have been worn through and through by her feet, down to the joust or beam. She is at this moment in good health.[5]

Female factory workers were either girls, childless spinsters like Betty Robinson, or single parents with one or more children to keep. At some factories, it was deliberate policy to prohibit the employment of married women. At Forbes, Low and Company, girls who got married were immediately dismissed. This rule was relaxed at the Donside factories, where married women were taken on temporarily as tutors to young operatives. This refusal to employ married women stemmed from ruling class opinion on the role of women within the home and the family. The rightful place of the married woman was in the home, looking after the needs of the husband, doing the domestic chores, and bearing and rearing children as a clean-living, responsible mother. However, it appears that unmarried women with children were not refused work in the factory. Such women were breadwinners, and respectable society considered it better to allow them work and wages than see them turned loose into the streets, with their children also at risk. Otherwise, within the family group, the husband was seen as major breadwinner, necessary for the preservation of his patriarchal authority, even if in reality the children were put out to factory work in the hope of keeping the family unit above the poverty line. And although there is ample evidence to show that several members of families were engaged in factory work in Aberdeen, there were few instances of 'factory families' in the full meaning of the term. Nevertheless, the division of labour demanded by industrial capitalism in textiles was instrumental in breaking up the family unit and traditional domestic relationships, and in this sense the factory proved to be a disruptive force.

An analysis of the division of labour within industrial capitalism would be incomplete without an account of its impact upon the profession of hand-loom weaving, one of the traditional male craft occupations. The story of its decline and social consequences has been well documented, and is rightly regarded as a classic casualty of increased competition, mechanisation, and the factory system of production.[6] The nature and results of these changes among Aberdeen hand-loom weavers and their families by the 1830s and 1840s are painfully clear. In the early decades of industrialisation, the introduction of power-driven spinning machines was a great boon to hand-loom weavers, giving them regular work and prosperity. William Thom recalled the early years of the nineteenth century when artisan weavers were labour aristocrats:

> Then was the daisy portion of weaving—the bright and mid-day period of all who pitched a shuttle, and of the happy one whose luck it was to win a weaver's smile. Four days did the weaver work—for then four days was a week as far as working went—and such a week to a skilful workman brought forty shillings. Sunday, Monday, and Tuesday were of course jubilee.
>
> Lawn frills gorged freely from under the wrists of his fine blue, gilt-buttoned coat. Weaving continued gradually on Wednesday.[7]

The palmy days came to an end with the successful introduction of power loom weaving within the factory, in Aberdeen from the mid 1820s. At this point there were about 3000 hand loom weavers in the locality, but by the early 1830s the number had fallen away to 1400, most of them leading a miserable existence on scarcely 5s. a week. The appalling plight of the domestic weavers was revealed in the evidence given before a parliamentary enquiry in 1834, where the destructive impact of the factory system upon their livelihood was highlighted by the Aberdeen spokesman, Lawrence Don.[8]

In the cotton industry he told how the introduction of steam-power looms at Woodside cotton works had crushed out the domestic weavers by undercutting the price of their piece work. These depressed men were wearing themselves out working over fourteen hours a day trying to compete with the new machines. Moreover, according to Don, the weavers considered themselves the victims of 'a vicious combination of masters'. Here, he pointed to three big firms, namely, Gordon, Barron and Co, Leys, Masson and Co (Grandholm), and Milne, Cruden and Co, and accused them of conspiring to reduce capital costs by wage-cutting and by lengthening the size of the webs given out to the weavers, without extra payment for the work and time involved. In desperation, weavers were forced to engage their women and children to learn to work the loom. This had the opposite effect to what they intended, as the weaving trade was overrun by incomers who had no option but to accept the prices of labour dictated by the leading firms. Thus weaving as an independent craft was diluted and destroyed while the power loom reigned supreme. Few men would accept factory work as operatives, particularly craft weavers who considered it a degrading form of work, but with the greatest reluctance some of them made the necessary transition from the hand loom into the factory premises where they did heavy linen weaving, while women were employed on the easier kinds of power weaving. These male linen weavers were aggrieved at the loss of the independence they had once enjoyed in the good years of the hand-loom weaving, even if the rates they earned at factory work were higher than they could fetch when the trade was depressed. Male carpet weavers at Hadden's factory in the Green were in a different category from other classes of weavers in that they could command regular work and good wages in an expanding home market throughout the 1830s, although they also were to share the same fate as their fellow textile workers in the depressions of the 1840s.

4

CONDITIONS ON THE FACTORY FLOOR

I go not beyond Aberdeen with its wet work—its night work—its mills and steam-boilers—its teeming numbers of living female machinery—its masters set over them, looking upon them only as such.

taken from an article condemning the factory system, in an Aberdeen weekly newspaper *The Banner*, 9 Jan. 1841

The textile factories of the industrial revolution violated all decent standards of health and safety. As places of work, the worst of them were hell holes, and even the best were dehumanising in their effect upon the workers. The factory system in Aberdeen contained all the evils associated with bad working conditions: low wages, long hours, extreme temperatures, dust and oil pollution, unboxed machinery, lack of immediate medical facilities, inadequate and sometimes non-existent facilities for changing clothes, washing, and eating meals; and a rigid, ruthless work discipline which gave rise to abuse and brutality.

While it is difficult to pinpoint with precision the actual conditions of work in each type of factory, it is possible to observe certain differences. The Bannermill was no model factory, but compared to all the mills and factories in the area, it had, from the start, exceptional facilities designed to create a modicum of decency in the workplace. Factory inspector, overseers, and workers alike noted its positive features. Built in 1826, this cotton mill was believed to be 'in all its parts, of the most approved construction; that great attention has been paid to the convenience, comfort and health of the workers by keeping the preparing room free from dust, by having large dressing and undressing rooms on every flat, by having separate water closets in each flat, by having a water pipe of drinking water in each apartment, by giving the workers abundance of room for their work, and having the machinery well fenced'.[1] There was a spacious room for eating meals which the workers brought in, a subscription library, and a sick fund, both managed by themselves. Thomas Bannerman and partners adopted a paternalistic attitude towards their workers, but nevertheless ensured that the workers were kept firmly in their place and disciplined to produce the maximum in efficiency and profitability for the masters. Aware of worse working conditions in neighbouring factories, the Bannermill workers who gave evidence to the 1833 Factories Commission complained only of long hours, but otherwise considered themselves reasonably fortunate.

The factory regimes at Donside had little to commend them, but by the 1830s and 1840s several of the works there had introduced canteen facilities on the premises. In contrast, none of the works in the city made this provision. Factory workers in the town either went home during the lunch break, or else ate soup and potatoes in the workplace. As many of the Woodside workers lived some distance away from their work, it was impossible to go home at meal time. Pirie and Co worsted mills installed a kitchen and prepared meals by the early 1830s, but neither the Grandholm nor the Woodside Works followed suit until the 1840s. The Grandholm plan, in particular, won high praise from the assistant inspector of factories in his 1847 report.[2]

The limited benevolence and paternalism shown by factory masters like Bannerman, Hadden and Kilgour were concessions which failed to lighten the oppressive burden of the factory system as it bore down upon the worker. There were factory masters in Aberdeen who did not begin to show any special regard for their workers. Here, the most notorious working conditions and regimes were to be found in the linen mills of the city, namely at Broadford and at Milne, Cruden and Co, Spring Garden. At these works, girl flax spinners had to endure atrocious conditions and treatment.

Female flax spinners worked on either dry or wet frames. The girls attending the wet frames were exposed to constant sprays of hot and cold water ejecting out from the spindles. At the Grandholm, the girls were given leather aprons to protect their fronts from the water, but at the other flax mills the girls had to supply their own protective clothing. Many of them could get only coarse linen aprons which were of no use as they absorbed the water. Girls employed in hot wet spinning departments were exposed to the additional health hazard of steam and of temperatures above 100 degrees fahrenheit. With water on the floor, the girls stood in wet shoes, or went barefoot. If they wore pattens or wooden clogs, they had to buy their own. Both factory commissioner and inspector responsible for

The Bannermill (1826–1904). Established by Thomas Bannerman on the "Sandy Lands" adjoining Queens Links. Site, off Beach Boulevard, now occupied by Northern Farmers Ltd.

the Aberdeen areas were convinced that wet spinning was the most unhealthy and unwholesome branch of linen manufacture and condemned the owners for disregarding the abominable conditions in which the girls had to work. The reported testimonies of the girls are explicit and harrowing; the following samples being taken from the evidence given to the Factories Commission of 1833.

Catharine Macintosh, aged seventeen, employed for ten years in the wet spinning room at Spring Garden 'has all along been very subject to coughs and colds, and she seldom sleeps with sore throats, and is getting very deaf; her feet and legs are so severely swelled that she can hardly walk; that she was in the infirmary a great part of the summer owing to illness brought on by wet spinning, and she thinks it a shame to set people to such work; that the wooden clogs save them a little from the wet, but they hurt their feet'.

Beatrice Morrison, aged twelve, also at Spring Garden, for three years in the first flat of the wet spinners 'has always been very hoarse since she was a wet spinner, and always stands barefooted on the wet stone pavement; that her feet and legs are so swelled that she often cannot put on her shoes, and she is plagued with a stitch in her side.'

Catherine McKenzie, aged twenty-two, at Broadford, and a cold wet spinner for twelve years, 'is seldom free of cold, and is very generally hoarse; that the cold wet spinning frame is more easily managed than the dry, but is not so comfortable.'

Also from the Broadford, Barbara and Jean Wood, sisters aged seventeen and fourteen, two years at the hot wet spinning frames, testified 'that their feet are constantly wet, and the front of their bodies from the waist downwards in the same state; that they have to dip their hands in hot water frequently; that they are never free from cold, are so hoarse that they have lost their voice, and that their hands are hacked in the winter'.[3]

Factory legislation by mid-nineteenth century offered no protection against general or specific health hazards which faced wet spinners and other textile workers. The 1844 Factory Act dealt with the fencing of dangerous machinery and thus offered some protection, but mitigation or removal of health hazards was left to the discretion of the masters, most of whom did not take the trouble and expense. Factory inspectors could exert some pressure on owners and at least in one instance inspector James Stuart appears to have persuaded a mill owner to bring in a modest improvement, when, in 1846, wet spinners at Spring Garden at last gained the benefit of splash boards to keep their bodies and the floors free of water.[4]

In the following chapters it should become clear how limited the scope of factory legislation really was in relation to conditions of work, and how much the worker was at the mercy of owners and the system. It ought to be realised that employers were still entirely free of government controls concerning fundamental issues such as wage levels and payment of compensation for industrial injury. According to the prevailing climate of 'laissez-faire' opinion, wages were dictated by the operation of 'free' market forces. On the other hand however, any attempts made by workers to win wage increases or other improvements by methods of collective bargaining were countered by a battery of statute and common law which protected the economic and class interests of the masters.

5

HOURS OF WORK AND THE CHILD LABOUR ISSUE

It was quite impossible for the young workers to devote any time to their education after leaving the mill, so thoroughly fatigued as he saw them; that they became sleepy in the evening, and he had continual difficulty to keep them awake, for if they had been found asleep the overseer would have been severely blamed; that he remembers one instance of a young female child being brought to the mill of Messrs Richards and Company (Broadford)—she was so young that the general remark was, she was fitter for her cradle than for the work; that she used frequently to fall asleep, and he felt so much for her that he allowed her to remain undisturbed, and the rest of the girls, who felt in a similar way, did her work for her in the meantime; that the mothers of the young female workers used to tell him that their children came home so worn out that they could hardly get them to eat their supper before they went to bed.

> evidence submitted by James Gillespie, former overseer at Grandholm, Spring Garden and Broadford, who himself was forced to leave factory work through ill-health. *Factories Enquiry Commission. First Report,* 1833

We, the undersigned ministers of the Gospel in the city of Aberdeen and its vicinity, do hereby express our approbation of the Bill introduced into Parliament by M T Sadler, Esq. for ameliorating the condition of the working classes in manufacturing establishments, in as far as said Bill proposes to prevent the employment in mills and factories of children under the age of nine years, and to limit the hours of actual labour for youth under eighteen years of age to ten hours a day, that is, allowing the usual and necessary two hours for refreshment and rest, from six a.m. till six p.m. We are induced thus to record our sentiments, because we cannot, as Christian clergymen, give sanction to a system such as now prevails; a system by which tender infants are subjected to labour beyond their strength in a polluted atmosphere, and that too for a longer daily period than the adult felon or the West India slave. We are further convinced, from our clerical experience, that the present long confinement of young persons in mills and factories is prejudicial to their morals, inasmuch as religious instruction cannot be adequately obtained; to their mental culture, inasmuch as no regular system of education can be pursued; to their health, inasmuch as constitutional debility and disease are entailed. Given at Aberdeen, this 25th day of May 1832.

> Petition signed by 29 Aberdeen clergy of all denominations in support of Michael Sadler's Bill; reproduced in the evidence submitted by Revd. Abercrombie Gordon to the *Select Committee on the Factories Bill*, 1832

Before the Factory Act of 1833, there was no effective legislation regulating the length of the working day in textile factories. In theory and in practice, the masters could work their labour force until they dropped. Moreover, it must be borne in mind that the 1833 Act dealt only with the hours worked by youngsters from the ages of nine to eighteen, whereas legislation on the working hours of adults was not won until 1844 for women, and until 1847 for adult males.

In the first half of the nineteenth century, Aberdeen factory workers were on a six-day week, with Sunday off. Standard clocking-in time was 6 a.m. to begin a working day of around 12½ hours, excluding stops for breakfast around 9 a.m. and for a midday break about 2 p.m. Break times varied in length from place to place; ranging from 20 minutes to 45 minutes for breakfast, whereas the dinner break was usually longer, ranging from 45 minutes to 1½ hours, but an hour at most factories. The time for stoppage of work in the evening again varied from place to place, but on or around either 7.30 or 8 p.m., after which time the workers could begin to pack up and go home. This arrangement applied to the city as well as the riverside works, with Gordon, Barron and Co, Broadford and Poynernook factories all shutting down at 8.05 p.m., and Gordon's Mills half an hour earlier. The Bannermill was the only exception to these times, stopping at 7 p.m.; and on Saturdays it stopped at 4 p.m., slightly earlier than at the other mills where work was carried on until 5, 5.30, or even to 6 p.m.

Before 1833, the actual normal working week in textile factories was never less than 72 hours, apart from the Bannermill which, from December 1832, had reduced the working week by 2½ hours without production loss or wage cuts. These long hours also applied to factory children who had no childhood in the accepted sense of the term, and, as far as can be ascertained from the evidence, neither they nor the adult workers were allowed more than two days' holiday in a year, plus Christmas and New Year.

Beyond the normal working routine, occasions arose when overtime work was required. For instance, all the factories made up for 'lost time' caused by breakdown of machinery, waiting for repairs, changes in gearing, or any other unusual occurrence. Secondly, when orders were plentiful, the workers were obliged to continue for up to an hour extra on alternate days. Examples of such practices were understood to be compulsory unpaid overtime, even if the worker continued to be paid by the piece during these overtime periods. However, on occasions when there was a shortage of yarn, spinners were paid overtime money for producing the necessary supply beyond their normal hours. The rewards for accomplishing these extra tasks were extremely poor, if we are to judge from the story of a 12-year-old spinner, Catherine Murray, from the Woodside Works. Twice, she and others had worked from six in the morning until ten at night to produce emergency quantities of yarn, each time being paid an extra 2d. for their efforts.[1]

Many Aberdeen factory workers were also subjected to long hours of night work, a practice which was even more exhausting and debilitating than the evils of daytime working. The Donside mills, dependent on water-power, often worked the machinery during the night and early morning. This was not done regularly throughout the year, but at times when the level of water was adversely affected by summer and autumn droughts, or temporary ice blockages in winter, causing a loss in production. At such times there was only enough water power to drive a small wheel, and a portion of the work force was organised for night shifts, so that production schedules could still be met. At the riverside mills, it was mostly youngsters—spinners and piecers—who were involved in night work. For example, at Gordon's Mills in the 1820s and early 1830s, 40 or 50 young workers did stints from 8 p.m. until dawn, with a half-hour break; and at the adjacent worsted spinning mill, one-fifth of the workers there did 10-hour stints with the small water wheel giving enough power to drive one-third of the machinery.[2]

At the Woodside Works and at Pirie's worsted mill, elaborate shift work schedules were devised to cope with the deficiency of water during certain parts of the year. Punishing broken shifts were introduced, so that, on a particular day, one group of workers started at 5.30 a.m., and broke off for three hours in the middle of the day before returning to work on until 9 p.m. Those who did the night shift got the whole of the next day off, and then returned on the morning of the following day to start on a new shift rota.

Patrick Pirie asked even more from his night shift workers at such times, namely to continue working through into the next day when it was possible to take advantage of sudden rises in the water level. As Pirie explained:

> The circumstances that occasion the regular hours having to be at times exceeded arises chiefly from the changes in the state of the river. For instance, when it rises at a time we are working during night, so that there is sufficient power to drive all our machinery at the hour of the morning the hands leave off, they continue to work, after being allowed time to wash and to take breakfast till noon or 2 pm, when they go home.[3]

Acknowledging that this was a punishing arrangement, he told the enquiry that he was careful to order his manager and overseers 'to work no child or any servant more than they can bear'. Still anxious to create a genuine impression, he maintained that night shift workers had a better deal than day workers, having to work only 55 hours a week, 'receiving for this the same wages as if they wrought the other 17 hours. These hands thus enjoy 17 hours a week more than the others do for rest, recreation and education. It may also be observed that the whole time between Saturday night and Monday night is at their own disposal.' However, if Patrick Pirie thought he was a generous employer, there are indications that some of his workers at least had a different opinion about the work arrangements. One 17-year-old yarn twister from his mill 'works generally through the summer, after the water begins to dry up, all night. Would sooner work during the day'[4]

Fitted up with steam power, the factories in the town avoided the problems of their riverside competitors and therefore did not share their reasons for carrying on night work. Only Hadden's woollen factory in the Green and the flax mill at Broadford had experimented with night work. This was in the early 1820s, but was abandoned apparently because several years of bad trade had depressed market prices, and was too expensive in running costs. One inevitable result of long working hours was fatigue, which made the worker listless and careless, and therefore more accident prone; and, as the medical report from the royal infirmary confirmed in 1833, 'since night working was given up, the number of accidents has diminished very considerably'.[5] It would have been no consolation to these young factory workers who had suffered the crushing of fingers and arms to read that stone quarries had now replaced textile factories as the places which produce the most serious accidents in the area.

For spinners, weavers, reelers and piecers, there

The "Barracks". A castellated building erected, 1797, near Persley Bridge by Gordon, Barron and Co. of Woodside Works as a dormitory for apprentices.

was no respite so long as the machines were going. Their long working hours were spent standing, and their rhythm of work was dictated by the pace of the machinery, which, by the 1830s, had been geared up to maximum speeds. In this situation, the operatives were mere 'living machinery'. Young workers who were bobbin carriers and shifters did have an opportunity to take rests, and if, at times, they had little to do during some parts of the day, the long confinement in the mill often exhausted them to the point of falling asleep. It is little wonder that those factory children who attended schools after their long day's work were in no state to learn anything. One school teacher at Woodside told the Commission that thirty children attended his school, 'but not regularly; they are sometimes working all night. When they do come, they are just stupified with bodily exhaustion and the noise.' Other school teacher witnesses, including ones from the city, complained in the same vein about their pupils from the factories.

The most scandalous features of child exploitation in factories were not removed until the passing of the 1833 Factory Act. Although its scope was limited, it proved to be an important piece of legislation, establishing the practice of government intervention in matters of employment, and its enforcement by paid inspectors. It banned masters from employing children under the age of nine, and reduced the working day of 9–13-year-olds to 8 hours, with a further 2 hours to be set aside for schooling. This Act also put an end to night work for all workers below the age of eighteen, and thus cancelled out one of the worst evils of the factory system.

Predictably, these positive steps towards state regulation of the working hours of children and juveniles were resisted by factory masters all over the country. From 1830 onwards, various groups of reformers, including Evangelical churchmen, humanitarians, and working-class organisations, campaigned against child slavery in the mills, and put pressure upon Parliament to bring in legislation to reduce working hours. In particular, the popular demand for a ten-hour day, as proposed in Michael Sadler's bill before Parliament late in 1831, raised a storm of protest among factory masters who objected to any interference in the operation of their business affairs.

In the two enquiries preceding the Factory Act, they elaborated their views in no uncertain manner, the Aberdeen masters taking a full part in the opposition to changes. All of them reacted to the proposal to reduce hours to 10 per day, spelling out ruin to themselves, the workers, and to the interests of the country as the leading manufacturing nation in the world. Their thinking was expressed in crude economic terms, and may be summed up briefly. Shortening the hours of labour to such an extent would inevitably result in a loss of production, which in turn would raise the costs of production and endanger existing profit levels, and markets would be lost to foreign competitors whose governments did not restrict the length of the working day, thus giving them an advantage over their British rivals. The tightness of competition could not permit concessions to the labour force in hours or in wages.

Of the Aberdeen masters, only Thomas Bannerman did not subscribe to these hard-line views in their entirety. As mentioned earlier, he had already made a slight reduction in working hours at the Bannermill and had proved to his satisfaction that the output and productivity of his workers had not suffered. He and Thomas Hadden were in favour of uniform legislation to bring about a slight regulation of working hours, but only if such legislation could be made binding upon all factory masters. They were sceptical about this anyway, and even they considered that a 12- or 11½-hour day should be the norm for all workers. Thomas Hadden was the only master to declare an opinion concerning an acceptable age limit for a child factory worker, and he was prepared to manage with workers from the age of twelve upwards. On the specific issue of shorter hours of work for youngsters, none of the factory masters would make this an exception. Their objections were argued on various grounds. Assuming all the time that the hours of adult workers should remain unrestricted, the masters objected to greatly decreased working hours of the young to around 6 to 8, arguing that two shift relays of youngsters would be needed to work with adults on a single long shift. In these circumstances, two sets of youngsters would have to be paid instead of one. It was seen not only as a matter of greater wage bills: Thomas Hadden thought it unlikely that an additional supply of young workers could be found to make up an extra relay team, and judged the proposal to be unmanageable due to the shortage of labour among this age group; and James Kilgour expressed the opinion of several masters that two shifts of young operatives was inefficient and detrimental to smooth production, as time would be lost in cleaning machinery for the incoming shift. Moreover, the training up of a new set of young operatives was thought to be impracticable as well as costly. Finally, Kilgour and other Donside masters who used water power rejected proposals to end night working, insisting that they were a special case requiring the continuing use of youngsters on night shifts during certain times of the year. Since 'the greater part of the machinery was not intended to be worked by full-grown persons'.[6]

These freely-expressed opinions and apologetics coming from the factory masters could not be easily countered by the workers. None of the Aberdeen workers giving evidence to the commission voiced fundamental criticism of their masters, although they sometimes plucked up the courage to protest about the long hours of work. Deterred and intimidated, they were afraid to express their real feelings about such matters. This much is clear from the statements of two overseers from Poynernook and Spring Garden. John Miller, from the flax works, said that his workers would all like shorter hours, 'but they did not petition'; and the Poynernook man, voicing the same opinion, claimed that the workers there 'did not choose to take any step for fear of consequences'. However, overseer James Begg, also from the Poynernook factory, was not deterred. His evidence incriminated the cotton masters. Asked 'whether he knows that a system of intimidation on the part of the proprietors of this mill, to prevent candid answers being given to the Factory Commissioners, has prevailed, and called upon on oath declares, that he does think such a system has prevailed, and that anyone giving an opinion to the Commissioners in favour of shorter hours would, if it became known, be turned off', does indicate the manoeuvres of at least one firm to suppress evidence. His statement was corroborated by a woman from the factory. She wanted shorter hours, 'but dinna mention it, for they would be angry'.

Nevertheless, few workers, irrespective of age, could disguise their heartfelt desire for shorter hours. Some complained about 'being forced to make up', namely to work compulsory overtime. Mary Milne from Grandholm told how 'the people are always talking about the length of the hours'.[7] Typically, many were anxious not to suffer a drop in wages if hours were reduced. Others, on the verge of despair, knew no option. For example, a distraught flax spinner from Broadford, troubled with a 'great cough' and swollen feet and legs, was desperate for shorter hours, even with less wages.

Although not all cowed and submissive, factory workers were at this stage still in the grip of the masters. Without trade unions or any form of organisation they were powerless to resist the masters and therefore did not exist as a force for collective protest. In the absence of a workers' movement, the local clergy were in the forefront of the agitation for factory reform in the years 1830–33. Led by the Evangelical minister, Abercrombie Gordon, the Aberdeen clergy organised petitions and public meetings for shorter factory hours and schooling for young workers. Their criticisms of the factory system were based upon moral and religious considerations, and their primary concern was to safeguard the rising generation and the community at large from religious destitution, depravity and crime. They indicted the factory system for failing to provide the means for religious instruction without which young factory workers would inevitably become godless, corrupt, undisciplined and irresponsible adults and a danger to the existence of civilised life. Long hours into the evening and night work in particular allegedly exposed young workers to sexual immorality and permissiveness, encouraging conduct which put them beyond the reach of God's saving grace. The clergy had little to say about the inhuman economic exploitation of children, and indeed considered that a ten-hour working day was not excessive for children over the age of nine or ten.[8]

The Factory Act of 1833 gave no protection to adult workers, and in some cases they were made to work even longer daytime hours with the assistance of two shifts of child helpers. In the Aberdeen area, masters had no difficulty in accommodating themselves to the new legislation. One notable outcome was the wholesale dismissal of young workers within the 9–12 age group, being content with the labour of teenagers who could do the same jobs for the same wages. Moreover, since the Act placed the onus on parents to arrange schooling for their children, the factory masters were under no such obligation to provide school facilities for any children and young workers in their employ up to the age of eighteen. Only at Woodside did the masters make an effort to provide schooling for their teenage workers, and in that respect they carried out the spirit of the law. The fate of the discharged 9–12-year-olds may be surmised. As needy parents had sent them out to factory work in the first place to make ends meet, other work had to be found for them in the absence of this source of employment in the textile industries. There was no legislation to prevent them from being employed at a host of occupations, and several are known to have found work at the two comb factories in the city, where the bulk of workers were very young, wages were lower and working hours longer than those of youngsters on day shifts in textiles.[9]

6

WORK DISCIPLINE AND ITS ENFORCEMENT

Industrial capitalism was a revolutionary system of production. As Marx showed, it broke down the 'Chinese walls' of the old economic order and opened up world markets to factory-produced commodities. It liberated the means of production and created great wealth for the masters; but it also created new forms of oppression by enslaving the workers in body and soul. Factory masters, operating in competitive markets, and committed to heavy capital investment in plant and machinery, demanded efficient and speedy production. The industrial labour force had to respond totally to that requirement. Operatives had to adapt their mental and physical faculties to the monotonous regularity of the machine and the tyranny of the factory clock. For this new class of workers, the work discipline of the factory system was an alien force, dictating the pattern of their whole life. It was a system which could not tolerate the life styles of workers recruited from peasant farming or craft workshop, small-producer backgrounds where some measure of independence and control over work practice and leisure was still exercised by the individual.[1]

The factory worker could not choose when to take a rest, to take a day or more off work and make it up later in the manner of the traditional hand-loom weaver or cobbler. Thus patterns of work which were irregular, seasonal, customary, diversified—all foreign to the factory system—had either to be given up, or placed under attack from all sides. In order to achieve the desired end of a docile and obedient labour force, the factory masters and their allies had to devise the means of enforcing firm discipline upon an unruly class, not only during their working hours, but at other times.

The task of exerting work discipline and social control among large numbers of industrial workers crowding into city and suburbs was a daunting one for the employers and for respectable society generally. There was no concerted strategy, and some disagreement within the ranks of the employing class as to the means of enforcing this control. For example, textile factory masters in the Aberdeen area were not openly and publicly involved in the temperance campaigns and crusades of the 1830s and 1840s. At first sight, this non-involvement in movements to root out alcohol and to encourage sobriety among the working population may be surprising, especially when drunkenness was associated with absenteeism and other irregularities which interrupted the work process. Temperance activists among shopkeepers, tradesmen, some of the clergy and self-improving workmen were scandalised by the prevalence of drinking and the laxity of the licensing laws which permitted over 200 premises and 'grog shops' to be open on Sundays in the early 1830s. Practices not conducive to work discipline included the frequency of social drinking among artisans and tradesmen. Tailors, shoemakers, hand-loom weavers and hecklers were notorious for gathering in regular drinking clubs and spending prolonged weekends in bouts of hard drinking; without doubt to find consolation and escape from their many problems.[2] However, examination of the teetotal and temperance movements in Aberdeen during this period reveals no indication that factory workers had the opportunity to meet in drinking clubs. At Woodside, calico printers had a bad reputation for drunkenness and loutish behaviour in the early years of industrialisation, but all this appears to have been stamped out or greatly reduced by the 1830s. An active temperance society at Woodside, headed by the parish minister, Revd David Forbes, claimed the credit for suppressing drinking habits there, putting on popular lectures, readings, musical evenings, and marquee soirees with food and soft drinks as alternative attractions. The Woodside lairds—who were also factory masters—would have welcomed this initiative, but, in common with the bulk of the clergy and other factory masters in the city, they were hostile to the strict, total abstinence movement which developed from the late 1830s. The Aberdeen Total Abstinence Society, with 3000 members in 1839, included many working-class radicals who practised and preached the principles of sobriety as an example to fellow workers to be thrifty, responsible, self-respecting citizens showing their fitness to exercise the vote and other democratic rights. To them, teetotalism was a political weapon, in contrast to the work discipline aspect which was the priority interest of the factory masters. To the masters, this anti-drink crusade was a platform for dangerous radicals and a popular movement outwith their control, dedicated to moral, social and political reform of a character

Broadford Works. Established at beginning of 19th century by Scott, Brown and Co. Passed, 1832, to present owners, Richards Ltd.

they could not support. A significant exception among factory masters in this respect was the prominence of the comb works owners as enthusiastic supporters of the movement. Stewart and Rowell, and John MacPherson were radical in their political views and promoted teetotalism among their workers for reasons of discipline and for working class self-improvement.[3]

However, in the 1830s and 1840s, the views of small comb factory owners did not count among the textile factory masters. Suspicious of and hostile to popular anti-drink movements, they chose to depend upon their own authority for the suppression of drunkenness at work. Exercising undivided rule in the factory, they had the power to enforce this discipline by immediate warning and dismissal as punishment on the spot for any serious infringements like disorderly behaviour arising from drink or other causes. Every worker on the factory floor knew that the master's code—explicit or implicit—carried severe penalties for incidents involving the consumption of alcohol; and conversely, that a reputation for sober and loyal conduct among capable male workers was a necessary attribute for favour and promotion.

Although there was only one 'factory school' in the whole Aberdeen area at any time until 1850 and beyond, the elementary school was an important agency for imparting work and social discipline and upright moral and spiritual values, particularly among children preparing to become factory workers. Since most factory workers did unskilled mechanical and menial jobs, masters did not need educated workers and schooling was regarded primarily as an instrument of control. Before the Factory Act of 1833, there was no effective legal provision for the schooling of factory children, and in Aberdeen it was the clergy who first raised the alarm about the dangerous prospects of ignorant, godless and criminal hordes of working class youth laying siege to the property and the values of respectable society.

Home mission initiatives carried out by Church of Scotland ministers did most to get children into the expanding number of Sunday schools which they opened from the turn of the century. By the 1820s the free Sunday school movement, supported by collections and legacies, had nearly thirty separate classes and teachers in the crowded central area of the city, catering for over 1500 children at any one time.[4] This part-time provision was the only formal schooling available to thousands of working-class and poor children. Sunday and weekday evening schools were sponsored by other denominations, including the Baptists, whose evening school in the early 1830s tried to provide for young mill workers from Broadford and Spring Garden.

Irrespective of the religious denomination, the quality of education was poor. It consisted largely of religious instruction, using the Bible as a reading book, with writing taught as a reward to the attentive. Bible reading and catechising was also the rule at the few Lancasterian schools set up in the city for reaching and teaching children of the labouring poor. Organised with young monitors, teaching was given free, or for small fees which working parents were encouraged to pay. William Thom in his short memoir recalled the existence of about fifty 'wifie squeels' (dame schools) at the time of his youth. Like the others in the city, the one he attended from a very early age was little more than a child-minding centre where working parents put their children during daytime. Older boys up to the age of nine or ten were fitted out with a Bible and Westminister Catechism in this ragamuffin college where the teaching of writing was impossible and little else besides.[5] Most children who went to day schools of any description were removed long before the age of ten, and sent out to work as wage earners for the family, many of them as factory fodder. Thereafter, the opportunities

of picking up the skills of reading and writing were left to chance and to self-initiative.

At dame schools or Lancasterian schools corporal punishment was administered severely and often. William Thom tells how the old dame used the tawse to expel her rheumatism and exercise her bad temper; while Thomas Edward at the Lancasterian school in Harriet Street was beaten by the master when barely six years old: 'his shirt was hard with clotted blood, and still sticking to his skin' when he returned home.[6]

Incidents like these may have been exceptional, but for children like Thomas who subsequently went to factory work, they could be the kind of chastening experience which encouraged ready submission to discipline on the factory floor, tamed before they arrived there. It is not recorded whether Aberdeen factory masters acknowledged their gratitude to the day schools which passed on their young pupils to the world of work or to the evening schools which endeavoured, largely in vain, to cater for those tired mill hands who struggled there after a long working day. This apparent indifference shown by many city masters was condemned by evangelical ministers, although Revd Abercrombie Gordon in his evidence to the Select Committee on the Factories Bill singled out Thomas Bannerman as an exception, noting his interest and support for elementary schools in the east end of the city.

Out at Woodside, the provision of elementary schooling for the industrial community was equally deficient, particularly in the early decades of industrial growth and settlement in the villages of Grandholm, Tanfield and Cotton. Woodside did not have a parish school until 1837, but the paternalistic factory owners and lairds had a little earlier supervised the opening of five small day and evening schools for mill workers, quarriers and their children. One of these buildings was a factory school, belonging to Gordon, Barron and Co. As a weekday school, also open in the evenings for youngsters coming off dayshift, and for religious instruction on Sunday, it was intended primarily for the company's own workers and for sons and daughters not yet old enough to go into the factory. Judging from the official factory reports, it would appear that the standard of teaching and provision, and the rate of attendance were higher than in the city, more young workers at Woodside showing that they could read and count. At Donside, the factory masters Kilgour, Hadden and Pirie seem to have pursued a more definite policy than that of their city counterparts in

their encouragement of free training in the 'habits of industry' from the infant stage. In this fashion, they undoubtedly sought to secure the loyalties of their workforce and a closer identity between worker and firm, from the bottom upwards.

Young mill workers going home in the evening found immediate release in displays of noisy banter along the streets, much to the annoyance of their social betters. Not to be denied a bit of fun and boisterous behaviour outside the factory walls, the workers knew the very opposite on the factory floor, where the methods of instilling and enforcing orderly conduct faced them at every turn. The way of keeping discipline on the factory floor may now be considered.

Beating of children was one of the main complaints brought against factory owners during the hearings of the first factory enquiries of the early 1830s. These accusations were true in many instances, and there are horrifying cases highlighting brutal treatment of young factory workers. There are, however, no known cases of systematic cruelty or physical assaults of such a serious nature in the Aberdeen mills, although one overseer from Woodside had known of incidents many years before where the strap was used against youngsters who were disobedient or neglected their work. It is precisely at this point that the evidence given before the enquiries has to be treated very carefully, as owners, managers, and overseers would not have voluntarily incriminated themselves, and workers—afraid of being victimised and dismissed—may well have suppressed the truth concerning the use and abuse of corporal punishment and other forms of violence. Nevertheless, it is still possible to arrive at certain conclusions on this issue, as it relates to the experience of Aberdeen factories.

The overseer from Woodside was probably correct in stating that strapping was a common enough occurrence in the earlier days of industrialisation, when young indentured apprentices were badly used; but, that in recent years, strapping was no longer being used as a means of enforcing dicipline on the factory floor. To a man, the Aberdeen factory owners gave sworn evidence in the early 1830s declaring that corporal punishment by tawse or any other instrument was expressly forbidden on their premises, clear orders being given to foremen and overseers, and that any found guilty of such misconduct were discharged or demoted depending upon the severity of the offence. Of course, how overseers conducted themselves among the workers outwith the presence of manager and owner is another matter, and they had opportunities to abuse the power which they possessed. It was also extremely difficult—and often impossible—for a young or adult worker to bring a case successfully before owner or law court. For example, Robert Seton, during his nine years as manager at the Woodside Works, had received only one complaint, concerning an overseer who had beaten a boy about the head with a strap. Seton had upheld the complaint, and merely persuaded the overseer to apologise to the boy. A similar complaint was brought before Patrick Pirie. He advised the overseer to pay £1 to the boy's father, hoping to keep the determined parent from pursuing the matter in the law court. The father took the case to law, lost, and had to pay all the expenses. Lastly, in his twenty-four years as manager at Grandholm, Alex Cooper reported of only one court case being brought against an overseer accused of physical abuse; the overseer being cleared of the charge, and paying a share of the court expenses. Apparently, the magistrates court scarcely gave nominal protection to an aggrieved worker, and the risk of incurring expenses was an obvious deterrent to any worker seeking justice from a legal system weighted so heavily against him.

If overseers were not permitted the use of strap or

stick, cuffing with the hand was a standard form of punishment, although some of the Aberdeen owners denied that they had ever sanctioned it in their codes of discipline. At the Poynernook cotton factory, for instance, the manager claimed that overseers were not allowed to 'push and shove' any of the workers, and one overseer from the same place understood that he was given the power to deliver the youngsters a 'lick on the side of the head to keep them to their work'. Witnesses from the workers at several factories said that they had got 'skelped' in this way, but nothing worse. The workers themselves generally agreed that 'bairns must be corrected or would not mind their work' and, when it was deserved, a slap was sufficient punishment. Spinners exerted this kind of discipline against their piecers, whether or not their child helpers were their own family; or, as the medical report from the Woodside Works put it: 'There is no punishment of a nature more severe than parental.'

However, when dealing with adult workers, other means of discipline had to be used. Physical restraints ranging from slapping to flogging may have created the desired effect on young workers who made up the bulk of the industrial labour force, but alternative and potentially more damaging sanctions were chosen in order to keep the adults in check. Misconduct of various kinds, however defined, whether wilful disobedience, or persistent lack of punctuality in arriving at work late in the morning, was generally punished by the imposition of fines or by dismissal. The threat of either form of punishment was sufficient deterrent to most workers who, as individuals, realised that they had no option but to concur with the rules laid down by their employers.

The imposition of fines was declared policy in the Aberdeen mills, although the Donside factory masters, who made no admission about this, may also have followed this policy. If the owners of the Woodside Works did not fine their workers at the Donside complex, they certainly did so at the hand-loom weaving premises in Belmont Street in the heart of the city. William Thom explained how it was used, and how disastrous it could be in its effects.

If, from whatever cause except sickness, a girl was absent, she was marked down and fined to the extent and in proportion to the time of her absence.

If she was late and after 7 a.m. she was not permitted to come in, lost the morning's work and fined a sixpence. Accumulated absence was punishable by deductions of 1s. per day, which, in some cases, meant that when she returned she worked for nothing until the fine was paid up. Earning an average of 6s. a week, no worker could afford to lose wages on the above scale of fines, and according to Thom, the prevalence of this harsh system drove factory girls to desperation and into prostitution.[7]

In the city's two flax mills, low wages were accompanied by the most severe oppression. At Spring Garden, workers were fined for being absent through illness, and, as at Belmont Street, one day's absence was penalised by the loss of two days' wages. Several workers testified that they went to work even when they were ill or unfit rather than risk the loss of wages or the grim reality of being sacked. At Broadford works, the mill girls were notoriously ill-treated. However, refusing to remain demoralised and sullen, they erupted into open revolt in the early part of 1834, demanding an end to the regime of oppression. Their chorus of grievances was expressed long and loud, and during the course of that strike they revealed the full extent of the arbitrary measures taken against them. An overseer from Broadford had already testified to the heartless fining of workers who were absent through illness and through other legitimate reasons. He had considered it 'an oppression and bondage, because it is a great punishment to be deprived of work and of one's daily bread', especially with 'a wife and family whom he must support'. John Lunham, a packing supervisor at Broadford was also extremely critical in his evidence. He deprecated the imposition of arbitrary fines, not only for being a few minutes late, but for the slightest inattention at work. Furthermore, he had the courage to speak out against the destination of these fines, which 'are not applied to any fund for the benefit of the workers, but go into the pockets of the employers'.[8]

All these points, and more, were repeated by the striking mill girls from Broadford, and girls from other mills expressed the same kind of grievances, as explained in a pamphlet published at the time of the strike. It asked a most pertinent question concerning the guarded character of the evidence given by workers to the Commission, compared to the freely expressed statements of girls at this later date:

It was certainly obvious from what they stated that there must have been something radically defective in the manner in which the Factory Commission conducted its investigations, when such abuses as those complained of could be allowed for a moment to continue.

A girl from the Bannermill stated that she had been fined 6d for singing in the Mill. Another, who had the misfortune to force a splinter of wood into her foot, was fined 6d for sitting down to get it extracted; and other two girls were also fined 6d each, for endeavouring to assist her in taking it out. A female at the same Mill was mulcted of a 6d, because the glue on the end of the bobbin at which she attended loosened; and she was thus compelled to pay for the time which was required in replacing it. About fifty persons from this Mill, and some other one, called out at the same time, that they were compelled twice a day to pay a fine of a penny for changing their clothes after going into the Mill, although only occupying them for five minutes at a time. Some were fined a penny for turning their backs to a frame; a penny for speaking to their neighbour; and twopence for reading a book!

During the relation of each of these complaints, more than 500 voices joined in asking "who get the fines that we pay?". Some complained of the foul language to them, and of being frequently knocked about and kicked![9]

The above catalogue of grievances reveals a more representative view of the regime inside Aberdeen mills and factories than can be obtained from the official sources. Asked about discipline, only one factory master, namely Thomas Leys Hadden, gave any indication of pursuing a policy which included positive discrimination in favour of rewarding good work and conduct with promotion to the best paid work. In this respect his flax mill at Grandholm was a progressive place compared to flax mills in the city. This example notwithstanding, it is patently obvious that managers and overseers, with or without the tacit agreement of the masters, used the 'stick' rather than the 'carrot' for setting and achieving the required standards of discipline.

7

INDUSTRIAL CONFLICT AND POLITICAL STRUGGLE

During the eighteenth century Aberdeen wool-combers had engaged in episodic struggles with their masters over piece rates and the right of combination. Hand-loom weavers were also involved in a running battle to protect their livelihoods from 1800, joining national campaigns to petition Parliament for a minimum wage and protesting in vain against the removal of apprenticeship regulations which allowed the trade to be invaded by any person who learned the easy technique of working the loom. Aberdeen weavers had taken part in the widespread Scottish strike of 1812, only to be beaten back by enforcement of the law and the imprisonment of the Glasgow leaders.[1] Thereafter sectional trade unionism among the weavers was impotent to prevent a drastic decline in their fortunes and the Aberdeen weavers were under constant pressure to seek out new strategies in order to survive as a profession.

It was hand workers who were involved in these early struggles; but until 1834, Aberdeen's factory workers were too oppressed to form combinations or to engage in collective struggle over wages and conditions. The factory masters had succeeded in imposing their own conditions. The highly paid male mule spinners at Woodside were unlike their militant brethren in Glasgow and Lancashire, and were probably too few and too isolated to conduct a sustained struggle to resist the plans of the masters to break down this male preserve and fill their places with the cheaper labour of women and girls.

When mill girls at Broadford suddenly left their machines to walk out on the morning of 7 February 1834, they were the first group of industrial workers to take strike action in the city. For five determined weeks, these women were in the front line of the working-class struggle, discovering and developing remarkable resources of collective action and solidarity with groups of male workers from the factories and also from traditional trades. A deep sense of grievance arising from the atrocious conditions and harsh disciplines inflicted upon workers at the coarse flax spinning mills of the city certainly contributed to the upsurge of resentment leading up to the strike, although it was not the cause of the industrial action. It began as a reaction to a reduction of wages, the latest in a line of reductions which had resulted in 2s. loss over an 18-month period. These cuts were imposed on spinners and reelers, wages at the Broadford mill being lower there than at any other flax mill. The intimation of a 6d. wage cut finally brought the issue into open conflict between the workers and Pellatt the manager.[2]

By the second day, the spinners were solid and the mill had to cease production. Quickly, a strike committee was formed from female operatives, male flax dressers and hand weavers employed by the company. A street demonstration and open public meeting was held to publicise their struggle and to raise funds for printing and circulating handbills among other factory workers in the neighbourhood. At a large evening meeting of over 1000 mill girls from the Aberdeen area, they decided to form an all-embracing Female Operative Union, inspired by the example of their sisters in the west of Scotland who had just formed a power-loom weavers' society and who were involved in a movement to unite workers in the textile trades to form a general union to fight against wage cuts and other grievances. A highlight of the Saturday mass meeting was the speech of Mary Brodie—a spreader at Broadford—who told how she had been victimised for refusing to blackleg on the reelers, had been manhandled for her obstinacy, and threatened with arrest and imprisonment in the Bridewell for disobeying the commands of the overseer. In a rousing speech, reported in the local press, she declared her profound belief in the necessity of trade unionism 'to protect ourselves against the unjust rapacity and abuse of our employers'.[3]

The demands of the strike committee were modest and consistent throughout, calling for a wage rise to put Broadford mill girls on a par with their sisters in other Aberdeen mills, and for the re-instatement, without victimisation, of all the strikers. As expected, Pellatt refused to recognise the strike committee and the broader organisation the Female Operative Union as legitimate representatives of the workforce. Pellatt insisted that the operatives on strike had been receiving 5s. 6d.–6s. a week in wages and 'whether high or low, the rate is established by the great law of supply and demand', thereby refusing to concede that the workers had a case.[4]

A strike fund—the 'sinews of war'—was organised to pay the wages of the locked-out Broadford women. Treasurers saw to the collection of subscriptions and donations from factories and workshops throughout the city and Donside. In this way, over 200 workers regularly got strike pay, acting upon the correct advice of the weavers' society who cautioned against rash escalation of the strike to other factories, thus avoiding the danger of over-committing their financial resources and bringing about a collapse of their struggle. As trade was brisk, they reckoned that none of the masters would be prepared to lose out to their competitors in the event of a costly strike, and that selective strike action at one workplace at a time was the best tactical weapon to use. In this, they made a shrewd assessment, although Pellatt held out for nearly five weeks before conceding the workers' wages demand. For their part, the strikers could never have held out had it not been for the remarkable display of financial and moral support given them by other trades. Particular support came from the shoemakers' and tailors' societies whose members were then in dispute with the masters over pay and conditions of work.

The journeymen tailors had struck work a short time before the Broadford action. They wanted shorter hours, a more healthy workshop atmosphere, and a reversal of the masters' policy of forcing through a change in the mode of payment from hourly rates to piece work, making it difficult for most workers to make a decent living.[5] The shoemakers—another prominent artisan sector—were also under pressure from middlemen and sub-contractors who employed cheap labour, and, like the tailors, retained a reputation for outspoken and radical opinions. They were not on strike, but helped to organise the conduct of the women's struggle, and participated in the moves to create general unionism among city workers.

In the course of the disputes and struggles which co-incided in the first part of 1834, a new dimension emerged in the consciousness of many Aberdeen workers. In February they came to develop an active interest in the collective ideal of general unionism as the instrument of struggle for paving the way to a more just society. Out of the various conflicts, industrial workers and artisans alike realised that the particular grievances of each occupation contained a core of common grievances arising from an oppressive system. This realisation above all was expressed at the time in the drive towards united action, as unity was strength. At a large Saturday evening meeting towards the end of February, workers declared their purpose 'of forming themselves into one general trades union and to co-operate in procuring the re-dress of all grievances'. After speeches from Francis Banks, secretary of the tailors' union and other workers, the meeting resolved to form such a body immediately.[6]

Such a significant step forward in the growth of trade union consciousness was certainly born out of the realities of local struggles, but the outburst of enthusiasm for both the practical realisation of trade unions and for the idealism of general unionism may have been generated in part by an awareness of the scheme, associated with Robert Owen, of building national unions federated into one giant organisation. At this particular time, the Grand National Consolidated Trades Union had several hundred thousand members in England, and had a kindred organisation in the west of Scotland.[7] In Aberdeen, the interest in general unionism was unfulfilled in practice, as was the intention to publish a weekly 'trades paper' for working-class readers. This failure to achieve little more than a momentary presence of general unionism in the Aberdeen locality can be traced partly to the collapse of the Grand National Consolidated Trades Union and the widespread demoralisation which resulted from its demise in the spring of 1834; but much more, to the local situation where the odds were stacked high in favour of the masters and their allies who were in a strong position to take punitive action against strikers and trade unionists.

The mill girls in particular were subjected to all kinds of threats and intimidation in attempts to influence them to renounce trade unionism and to return to work, Throughout the strike they conducted themselves with fortitude and self-discipline, and spent much of their time formed in classes where they learned reading, writing, sewing and other types of self-help activities. Moreover, they withstood the barrage of hostility thrown at them by the clergy, the *Aberdeen Journal,* and other bodies.

Every plan was tried, in a clandestine manner, by Pellatt and his tools, to break the strength of unanimity among the females; some were forced to their employment by the threats and remonstrances of their parents, by the wheedling of petty foremen. But this is not all; the Broadford millocracy have not been idle—they have acted their part in a manner becoming their station; for besides the assistance which the Clergy rendered to them—and the Gentlemen of the Cloth certainly deserve their best thanks—not a town in the south and north in which a manufactory or agency residence is established, but had due notice forwarded to them not to employ an Aberdeen weaver! A particular description of Messrs Donald and Thomson (leaders of the flax spinners and weavers respectively) have also been sent to most of the mill spinners in the south, and they are represented as dangerous demagogues! Now, after this, who will not acknowledge combination among mill owners?[8]

The *Aberdeen Journal,* weekly newspaper and organ of local Toryism, raged at the strike girls and their comrades. It tried to invoke parental authority against these 'misguided girls' led astray by 'idle and designing persons', and pretended to be shocked by the girls 'spending their evenings in misguided clamour at meetings in a tavern, of what is called the Aberdeen Female Union'.[9] It also tried to break the morale of the girls by spreading rumours about misuse of strike funds, and reminded them of the power of the law despite the 1825 Act giving freedom to the existence to trade unions.

David Thomson, the weavers' secretary, had warned the girls about the role of the ministers of religion. They were the same Aberdeen clergy who had petitioned and campaigned so vehemently against the scandal of child labour in factories. However, their philanthropic stance was confined to this issue, being totally opposed to any attempt made by workers to form independent organisations such as trade unions and to engage in struggles which flexed the muscles of labour's power to resist injustice at the place of work and outside it. The girls had 'particularly to be on guard against the representations of certain clergymen, who appeared to be in league with the manufacturers, and who, by working on the fears and superstitions of the females, sought in a manner to force them to return to work'.[10]

In the end, Master and Servant law had to be used as a more weighty instrument than the subtleties of the clergy. Pellatt conceded the wages claim of the spinners and reelers, but extracted revenge by operating the laws of contract against the workers who had defied him. Pellatt maintained that the women had violated their contract of work by leaving without giving due notice of doing so. The women denied that any such contract, written on paper, had ever been issued, and this would appear to have been the case at Broadford. The sheriff took the word of the factory master and issued discharge certificates to all the strikers who refused to return. As these documents recorded that the individuals concerned had been on strike, they were effectively put on the blacklist, which meant that there was no chance of finding employment at factory work in the city or elsewhere. These measures applied to strike leaders among the weavers and flax dressers as well as to those women and girls who were known as militants during the strike.

Victimisation of workers extended beyond Broadford. One interesting case, reported in the *Aberdeen Herald*, weekly Liberal paper, which took a neutral stance over the strike, involved a young spinner at the Bannermill. Sarah Copland had been sacked from work, being 'guilty of insubordination by circulating in the work a placard of the Female Union' and for attending 'a meeting of that Union in Roberts' Hall'. She fought back courageously and took her employer, Thomas Bannerman, to the Small Debt Court. She pleaded that the written contract of master and servant was a reciprocal agreement which required each party to issue six weeks notice in the event of a master wishing to dismiss an employee, and of a worker intimating an intention to leave. The sheriff conceded this point as a principle, and Sarah Copland got her missing wages, with expenses.[11] However, she was told that circulating placards at her work might alone have justified dismissal, and it is uncertain whether she remained much longer at the Bannermill.

Winning the wages battle at Broadford was achieved at heavy cost, as the Aberdeen Female Operative Union failed to survive the struggle. Its last service was to pay travel expenses of victimised mill girls who went to Dundee in search of work. Without organisation, further attempts to restore wage levels at Broadford or at any other factory were bound to be defeated sooner or later as the masters found opportunities to erode any short-lived gains made by the workers. During the periods of cyclical recession between 1836 and 1848, the textile industries were severely hit, and the masters resorted to various forms of attack upon the workforce. Faced with declining markets and drastic falls in profit rates, they imposed short-time working, wage cuts and redundancies. Factory workers were in desperate straits, and could offer only sporadic, ineffective resistance at the workplace. In August 1840, mill girls at all the linen works struck work, disgusted and dismayed by another wage cut. As in 1834, feelings ran high, and moves were made to form a strike committee and fund. Blacklegs were obstructed outside Broadford, but the strikers were starved back to work at a time of high food prices.[12]

Throughout the struggles of the 1830s, mill workers, weavers, tailors and shoemakers learned the hard way that trade unionism, industrial action and sectional activity all had limitations and were subject to defeat. However, such experiences proved to be necessary and valuable steps in the direction of seeking alternative initiatives in the abiding struggle for social justice. Having exhausted other means of struggle, they found themselves turning to political action with the development of the Chartist movement from 1838 onwards. Under the banner of the six points of the 'People's Charter' they campaigned for the vote and other democratic rights and aimed at control of Parliament to secure legislation to improve working conditions and living standards.[13]

In Aberdeen, the leading Chartist activists came from artisan trades like tailoring and shoemaking. Many of them already had a reputation for outspoken radical opinions and independence of mind, and could make time in evenings and at weekends for engaging in political activity. However, as we have seen, factory workers, and especially children and women, stood outside the world of political involve-ment, and worked long hours which prevented them from taking an active part in the political work of committees and meetings. Nevertheless, factory workers were prominent rank and file supporters of the Chartist movement, and could be relied on to attend mass outdoor rallies, to sign petitions, and even to donate some money. Moreover, there is enough evidence to show that female factory workers were the most prominent among their sex in their enthusiasm for the People's Charter, although little is known of their participation. Early in 1839, a Female Chartist Association was formed with mill workers among the members. And during the biting economic and social crisis in 1842, the Association increased its strength with a fresh influx of industrial workers from textiles and the comb works, holding weekly meetings and lectures. At the same time, they were joined in their support of Chartism by 120 flax dressers from Broadford and Spring Garden, after a spate of redundancies.

The depressed hand-loom weavers also turned to Chartism during the slump of that year. They were late in declaring their allegiance to political radicalism as the way out of their predicament. In adversity, they had clung stubbornly to craft sectionalism, retaining the proud mentality of their heyday as labour aristocrats, and shunned outright political demands and perspectives. They adopted instead a posture which was backward-looking, yearning and striving for the restoration of paternalist government legislation which had protected them in the past, but which had since been removed by the manufacturers' lobby in Parliament. Time after time from the turn of the century they had petitioned Parliament to establish a Board of Arbitration to regulate wages, prices, and trade practices in their interest, and in 1834 had voiced their last despairing cry against the symbols of their oppression—calling for a government tax on the hated power looms. Lawrence Don's evidence before the 1834 enquiry contained all these demands, but to no avail. He testified to the loss of self-respect among the weavers, their inability to continue to afford to educate their children, to the demoralisation which led many of them to drink and crime, and the dire prospects of pauperism ahead. He hinted at imminent rebellion among those who were not demoralised: 'There is something very material in their breasts.' Yet, even then, the bulk of the hand loom weaving community hesitated to unite with other sections of the working class in the common cause for the redress of grievances and held on to the hopelessly misplaced convictions of the past era.

Dramatically, in the summer of 1842, they finally turned to the politics of Chartism, when unemployment and hunger confronted them. At one July meeting, 'a large procession of hand loom weavers arrived at George Street Hall to obtain cards of membership' of the Chartist Union. They had already made additional sacrifices to help Chartist funds, 'the poor depressed weavers of Short Loanings' having donated 10s., and the Broadford weavers 14s. 2d. to finance the expenses of an Aberdeen delegate to attend the Chartist Convention in London. These gestures are a poignant illustration of the change in consciousness within an occupation group which hitherto had chosen to remain aloof from working class unity and political radicalism.

However, radical protest could not reverse the fate of the weavers. Again they rallied with other sections of Aberdeen workers in the last phase of Chartism in 1848; but, as in 1842, Parliament and the ruling class withstood the pressures of widespread mass agitation and the democratic movement was defeated.

The cyclical economic crisis of 1848 also sealed the fate of virtually all the textile firms which had been built up in the course of over a half century of industrial revolution. Complete collapse of domestic and international markets destroyed demand for textile products and the Aberdeen factories had to close their gates. The first disasters were reported in May, when Leys, Masson and Co and Hadden and Sons shut down and made 3000 workers redundant. Equally disastrous was the failure of the cotton sector, which had always suffered from the heavy competition of Lancashire and Lanarkshire. It never recovered and was obliterated from the local industrial scene. The Bannermill, the Poynernook factory and the giant Woodside Works were sold soon after. Grandholm also changed hands and from the late 1850s again began to specialise in the production of quality woollen cloth.

The economic crisis of 1848 was a watershed in the life of the industrial community. It signalled the end of the factory system as local people had known it. To the workers, the demise of the factory system, which had brought so much suffering to so many, was not even a consolation. Thousands of families were out of work for a year or more and had to accept the charity of soup kitchens, church collections and subscription funds until the shattered local economy began to revive. And when the textile industry restarted—a shadow of its former self—with a much reduced labour force of men, women and youngsters, its prospects were brighter during the buoyant years of the mid-Victorian boom. As before, however, Aberdeen textile workers had to find their own salvation. Whether in boom or slump, they had to endure within the capitalist system, still without rights as workers and as citizens, so that, sooner or later, the struggle for decent working conditions, living standards and democratic rights would have to be renewed.

NOTES

CHAPTER ONE

1   For urban extension and civic improvement in the early nineteenth century, there is good coverage in William Robbie, *Aberdeen: Its Traditions and History* (1893); in William Watt, 'Fifty years of Progress in Aberdeen', *Transactions of the Aberdeen Philosophical Society*, vol. IV (1910); and in part 4 of Alexander Keith, *A Thousand Years of Aberdeen* (1972)

2   *Robbie*, op. cit. p. 404; A S Cook, *Old Time Traders and Their Ways* (1902); pp. 79–80. and the delightful book by William Skene, *East Neuk Chronicles* (1905), p. 104.

3   Drs A Kilgour and J Galen, *Sanitary Condition of the Poor in Aberdeen. Sanitary Enquiry, Scotland* (1842). Also printed as a pamphlet.

CHAPTER TWO

1   A J Durie, 'Linen Spinning in the North of Scotland, 1746–1733', *Northern Scotland*, vol. 2 (1974–5); also A J Durie, *The Scottish Linen Industry in the Eighteenth Century* (John Donald) (1979); I C M Barnes, 'The Aberdeen Stocking Trade', in *Textile History* (1977).

2   The putting-out system as practised in Aberdeen and district is described in *Old Statistical Account*, vol. XIX, pp. 204–5. The *Statistical Account of Scotland* is out in a modern reprint, eds D J Withrington and I Grant.

3   Part 4, chapter 4 of Alexander Keith's book provides a useful rundown on local textiles.

4   Patrick Morgan, *The Annals of Woodside and Newhills* (1886), p. 30, the main secondary source dealing with industrial Donside.

5   Short article by G M Fraser, on Broadford and its owners, in *Journal of Aberdeen Chamber of Commerce* (July 1920).

CHAPTER THREE

1   *Factories Enquiry Commission on Employment of Children in Factories. Supplementary Report. Part II. Answers of Masters to the Central board of Commissioners (Parliamentary Papers 1833)*. Other quotations in this paragraph are taken from the same source.

2   Samuel Smiles, *Life of a Scotch Naturalist* (1889), pp. 47–51.

3   *Factories Enquiry Commission. First Report.* Evidence taken by Robert Mackintosh. *Parliamentary Papers 1833.*

4   *Factories Enquiry* (1833). *Answers of Masters,* op. cit.

5   *Factories Enquiry* (1833). *Supplementary Report.* Medical report by Sir David Barry to the Central Board.

6   The only full-length published study on weavers in Scotland is the important recent book by Norman Murray. *The Scottish Hand Loom Weavers.: A Social History 1790–1850.* Duncan Bythell, *The Hand Loom Weavers* (1969), deals mainly with the English scene.

7   William Thom, *Rhymes and Recollections of a Hand Loom Weaver,* ed. W Skinner (1880), p. 3.

8   *Select Committee on Hand Loom Weavers. Parliamentary Papers 1834.* Minutes of Evidence. Lawrence Don, Aberdeen.

CHAPTER FOUR

1   *Factories Enquiry Commission. First Report.* From the summary report by James Stuart. *Parliamentary Papers 1833.*

2   Mr Walker, assistant to James Stuart, factory inspector, visited the kitchen and canteen at Grandholm and wrote a long, glowing report on his findings. This included remarks on the food. Breakfast consisted of a roll of bread and coffee; mid-day dinner was barley broth or pea soup with bread, the soup being made with meat through it. Walker had tasted the food and thought it excellent. Breakfast and dinner cost 1½d. *Report Inspector of Factories* (June 1847). James Stuart, *Parlimentary Papers 1847* (Appendix No.3).

3   *Factories Enquiry* (1833). First Report. Evidence taken by James Stuart and Robert Mackintosh.

4   *Report. Inspector of Factories* (Nov. 1846). James Stuart. *Parliamentary Papers 1847.*

CHAPTER FIVE

1   *Factories Enquiry Commission. First Report,* op. cit.

2   *Factories Enquiry Commission. Answers of Masters,* op. cit.

3   ibid.

4   *Factories Enquiry Commission. First Report,* op. cit.

5   *ibid.*

6   *Answers of Masters,* op. cit.

7   These statements from overseers and workers are taken from the *First Report,* op. cit.

8   *Select Committee on the Factories Bill. Parliamentary Papers 1832,* pp. 214–26. Evidence submitted from Aberdeen by Revd Abercrombie Lockhart Gordon, 8 June 1832.

9   Child labour at the comb works was investigated by the *Children's Employment Commission, Parliamentary Papers 1843.* Minutes of evidence collected by R H Franks, east of Scotland.

CHAPTER SIX

1   See the seminal article by Edward Thompson, 'Time, Work-Discipline, and Industrial Capitalism', *Past and Present* (1967).

2   There is a considerable body of literature on temperance and teetotalism. A S Cook, *Pen Sketches and Reminiscences of Sixty Years* (1901), written by a temperance zealot, gives a good introduction to the movement in early nineteenth-century Aberdeen. The view of a self-improving worker and Chartist is revealed in William Lindsay, *Some Notes: Personal and Public* (1898), pp. 156–61.

3   *Aberdeen Herald* (13 Jan. 1844).

4   Robert Wilson, *An Historical Account and Delineation of Aberdeen* (1822), pp. 196–7. A Allan MacLaren, *Religion and Social Class: The Disruption Years in Aberdeen* (1974),

contains much informed comment on the Church and educational provision for the labouring classes and their children.

5 *William Thom,* op. cit. pp. ii–iii.

6 *Samuel Smiles,* op. cit. p. 41.

7 *William Thom,* op. cit. p. 4.

8 *Factories Enquiry Commission. First Report.* Evidence taken by James Stuart.

9 *Aberdeen Female Operative Union. Detailed Report of the Proceedings of the Operatives since the Turn-Out* (1834), published as a 1d. pamphlet.

CHAPTER SEVEN

1 W H Marwick, *Short History of Labour in Scotland* (1967), ch. 2. Ian MacDougall, *Labour Records in Scotland* (1978), p. 119 describes source materials concerning journeymen wool combers in late eighteenth-century Aberdeen.

2 *Aberdeen Herald* (8 Feb. 1834).

3 *Aberdeen Herald* (15 Feb. 1834).

4 *Aberdeen Herald* (22 Feb. 1834).

5 *Aberdeen Herald* (25 Jan. 1834; 8 Feb. 1834).

6 *Aberdeen Herald* (1 Mar. 1834).

7 G Oliver, 'The GNCTU. of 1834', *Economic History Review* (1964); also J F C Harrison, *Robert Owen and the Owenities* (1969), pp. 193–216; and G D H Cole, *Attempts at General Union* (1952).

8 *Third Report of the Female Operative Union* (1834) 1d. pamphlet.

9 *Aberdeen Journal* (5 Mar. 1834).

10 *Herald* (22 Feb. 1834).

11 *Herald* (1 Mar. 1834); *Third Report,* op. cit.

12 *Herald* (15, 22 Aug., 1840).

13 Many books and articles deal with the Chartist movement in Britain. Alexander Wilson, *The Chartist Movement in Scotland* (1970) is useful and includes some material on Aberdeen. Serious students should consult the provocative article by Stuart McCalman, 'Chartism in Aberdeen', *Journal of Scottish Labour History Society,* no. 2 (Apr. 1970). Robert Duncan, *Popular Radicalism and Working Class Movements in Aberdeen 1790–1850.* unpublished M Litt thesis 1976, concentrates on Chartism; as also does his article, 'Artisans and Proletarians: Chartism and Working Class Allegiance in Aberdeen 1838–42', *Northern Scotland,* 1981. Vol. 4, Nos 1–2.